Another Music

Through the Year

with

George Herbert

COPYRIGHT INFORMATION AND ACKNOWLEDGMENTS

This collection and its typography, artwork and layouts are
copyright © 2007 Summer Events with George Herbert Group
and Friends of St Andrew's, Bemerton.

All Rights Reserved.

Please do not photocopy any part of this book.

The copyrights of the music (unless otherwise specified) is owned by the composers and
administered by The Royal School of Church Music,
to whom all enquiries regarding reproduction should be addressed.

Order number: D0211
ISBN: 0-85402-164-7

Compiled and edited by Judy Rees, Barry Ferguson and Tim Ruffer
Music and typesetting by RSCM Press
Cover design by Sandi Ferguson

Published on behalf of Summer Events with George Herbert Group
and Friends of St Andrew's, Bemerton by
The Royal School of Church Music
19 The Close, Salisbury, SP1 2EB
Tel: 01722 424848 Fax: 01722 424849
Email: press@rscm.com Web: www.rscm.com

Contents

Advent
- Discipline — Barry Ferguson — 6
- Bitter-sweet — Barry Ferguson — 8

Christmas
- Christmas — Orlando Gibbons arr. Barry Ferguson — 9

Lent
- Denial — Simon Lole — 15

Good Friday
- The Sacrifice — Simon Lole — 18
- Longing — Barry Ferguson — 20

Easter
- Easter – Rise Heart — Barry Ferguson — 22
- The Dawning — Richard Shephard — 24

Pentecost
- Whitsunday — Grayston Ives — 26

Trinity Sunday
- Trinity Sunday — Barry Ferguson — 28

Sunday
- Sunday — Howard Moody — 30
- A True Hymn — Howard Moody — 32

Matins
- Matins — David Halls — 34

Evensong
- Evensong — Howard Moody — 35

General
- Perfection–The Elixir — Orlando Gibbons — 39
- The Pulley — Barry Ferguson — 40
- Gratefulness — Edmund Hampton — 43
- The Flower — Alec Roth — 44

Hymn commentaries by Canon Judy Rees — 46

PREFACE

Most church congregations know the hymns *Teach me my God and King* and *Let all the world in every corner sing*.

George Herbert, Rector of Fugglestone with Bemerton from 1630–1633, wrote those words and over 160 other poems. There has been a renewed interest in his life and work over the last decades, as people have been drawn to his poetic account of *the many spiritual conflicts that have passed betwixt God and my soul*.

Herbert's voice is a clear one. His poetry delights us with its artistry, its wit and its profound understanding of the relationship between God and human beings. We feel he knows from the inside the joys, anguish and complexities of responding to the love of God and following Christ. Herbert speaks to us today.

Since 2001, a group of neighbours in Bemerton have organised events to celebrate his life and work, and the idea of inviting composers to write hymn tunes for more of his poetry captured our imagination. We are grateful that each composer has responded with relish and skill, and want to record our thanks to them and especially to Barry Ferguson for his inspirational support and vital contribution since the beginning of this initiative.

Thank you to Mary Duncan who offered suggestions for some of the introductory paragraphs. There is an increasing range of literature about George Herbert for those who would like to explore further. *George Herbert-The Complete English Poems* edited by John Tobin and published in the Penguin Classics series, is a good place to start.

The Royal School of Church Music is now in the Cathedral Close of Salisbury. It has been a nice touch to travel the mile or so from Bemerton to the Close to work with the ever patient Tim Ruffer on this publication. George Herbert walked the distance twice a week, and called the time spent in worship at the Cathedral his *heaven upon earth*.

Judy Rees
Bemerton 2007

THE MUSIC

George Herbert's poetry soars. Any new music must also take wing, it seems to me.

How does one set about writing hymn tunes? A distinguished hymn tune composer told me that he first asks his collaborating text writer to produce the first verse only. He then composes a tune to match its metre and mood. The two of them meet and sing through, discuss and perhaps revise their work so far. When they are both completely happy, the writer produces all the following verses with the tune firmly in his mind. This ideal process is not now possible with George Herbert, alas! Instead a composer must somehow create, single-handed, a tune that fits and enhances every verse of the text.

Although Herbert loved and performed music, his poetry can present musical problems. Occasionally the number of syllables in a particular line varies from one verse to another. Or again: in the magnificent poem *Easter* the music for *With him mayst rise* (v.1) must also be sung to *And multiplied* (v.3): the first verse example benefits from an ascending phrase; the third verse example does not.

On the other hand one could argue that Schubert achieved miracles in his songs by simply repeating the same music for several verses. And many successful hymn tunes have been written after the text writer had died, and collaboration impossible. Hymn tunes require a 'broad brush' technique to catch the general mood, not each textual nuance. This is for me its fascination and its elusiveness.

In Greek mythology Bellerophon, another mere mortal, tried in vain to capture the divine winged horse Pegasus by many and huge exertions. Finally worn out, he fell into a deep sleep by a sacred stream, and was visited by the goddess of Wisdom in a dream. On waking he caught the animal without difficulty and soared with it high into the air. What does this teach us?

Barry Ferguson
Shaftesbury 2007

Discipline

MADDY

Barry Ferguson

JESSE CLOSE

Barry Ferguson

Copyright © 2007 Barry Ferguson

An adventurous scheme might be to sing 'Maddy' for verses 1–4, 6 and 7, and 'Jesse Close' for verses 5 and 8.

1   Throw away thy rod,
     Throw away thy wrath:
         O my God,
     Take the gentle path.

2   For my heart's desire
     Unto thine is bent:
         I aspire
     To a full consent.

3   Not a word or look
     I affect to own,
         But by book,
     And thy book alone.

4   Though I fail, I weep:
     Though I halt in pace,
         Yet I creep
     To the throne of grace.

5   Then let wrath remove;
     Love will do the deed:
         For with love
     Stony hearts will bleed.

6   Love is swift of foot;
     Love's a man of war,
         And can shoot,
     And can hit from far.

7   Who can scape his bow?
     That which wrought on thee,
         Brought thee low,
     Needs must work on me.

8   Throw away thy rod;
     Though man frailties hath,
         Thou art God:
     Throw away thy wrath.

Bitter-Sweet

BITTER SWEET

Barry Ferguson

1. Ah my dear an-gry Lord, Since
2. I will com-plain, yet praise; I

thou dost love, yet strike; Cast down, yet help af-
will be-wail, ap-prove: And all my sour-sweet

-ford; Sure I will do the like.
days I will la-ment, and love.

Copyright © 2007 Barry Ferguson

§ last verse tenor E♮

Christmas

EASTBURY SONG I

Orlando Gibbons
adapted and arranged by Barry Ferguson

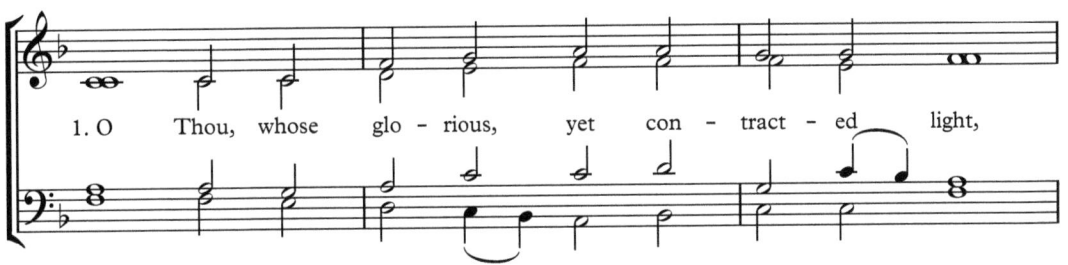

1. O Thou, whose glo - rious, yet con - tract - ed light,

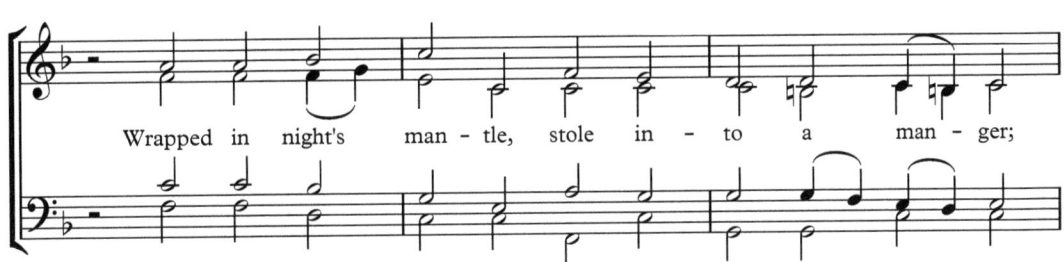

Wrapped in night's man - tle, stole in - to a man - ger;

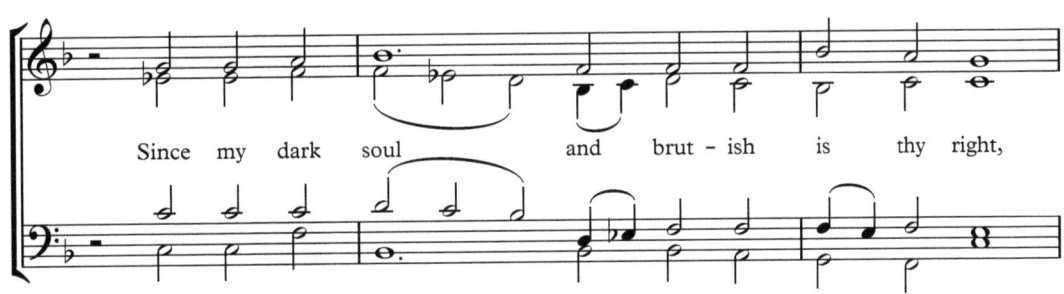

Since my dark soul and brut - ish is thy right,

To Man of all beasts be not thou a stran - ger:

Copyright © 2007 Barry Ferguson

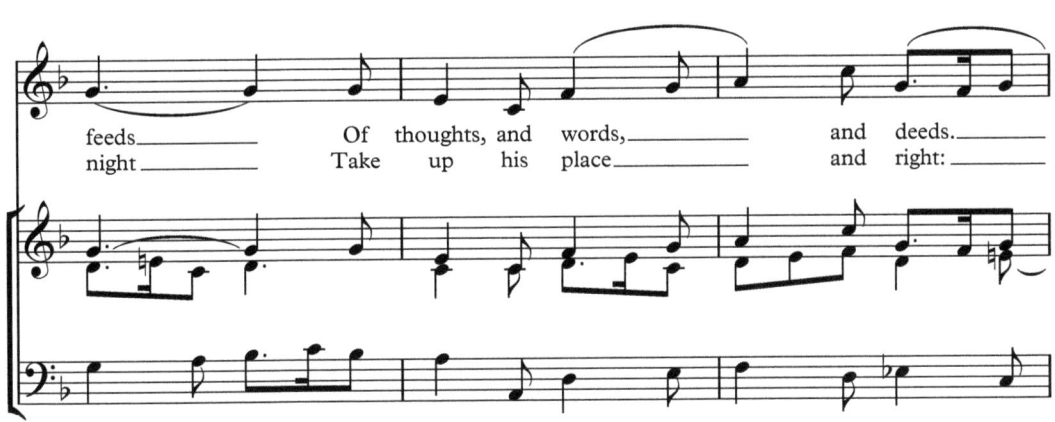

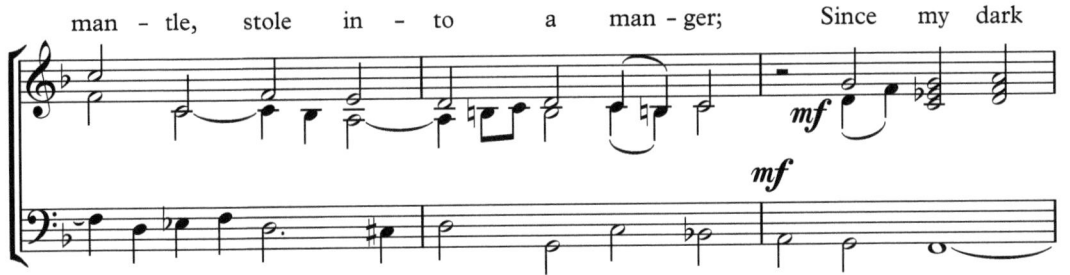

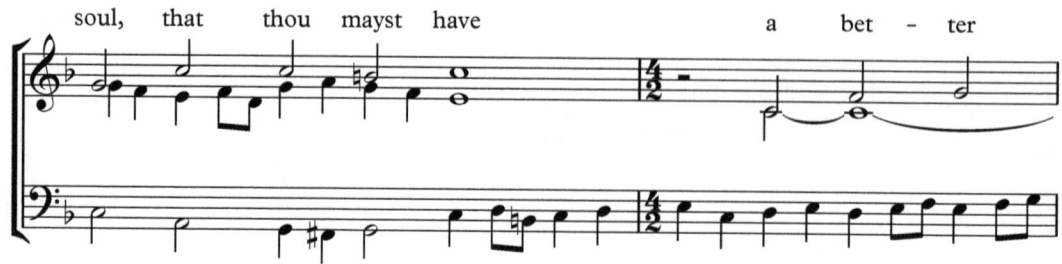
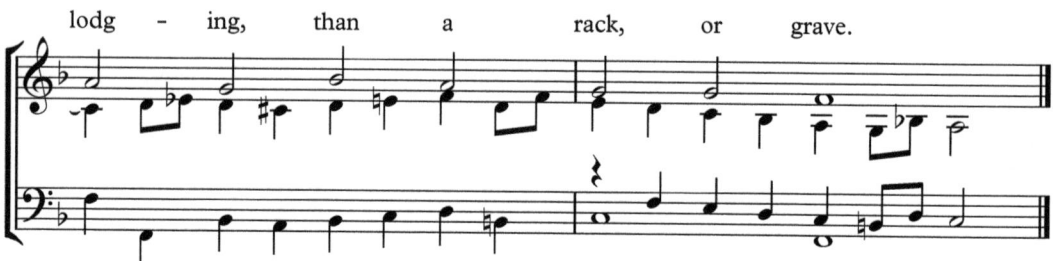

Denial
EAST KNOYLE

Simon Lole

1. When my de-vo-tions could not pierce Thy silent ears;

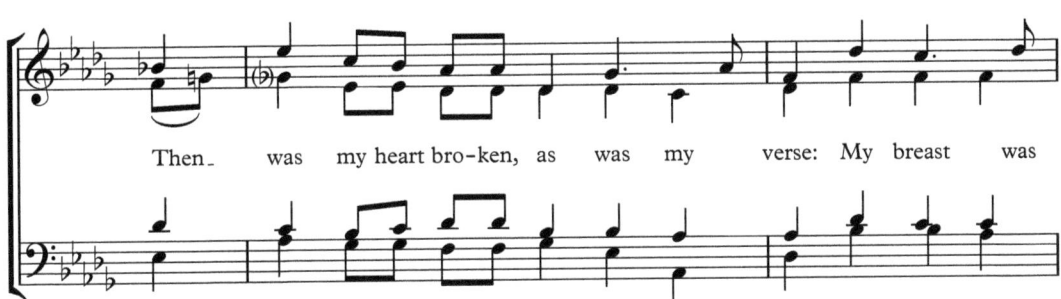
Then was my heart bro-ken, as was my verse: My breast was

full of fears And dis-or-der.

2. O that thou shouldst give dust a tongue to cry to thee,

© 2007 Simon Lole.

The Sacrifice
HIGH PEAK

Simon Lole

© 2007 Simon Lole

1   O, all ye, who pass by, whose eyes and mind
        To worldly things are sharp, but to me blind;
        To me, who took eyes that I might you find:
              Was ever grief like mine?

2   Betwixt two thieves I spend my utmost breath,
        As he that for some robbery suffereth.
        Alas! what have I stolen from you? Death:
              Was ever grief like mine?

3   A king my title is, prefixt on high;
        Yet by my subjects am condemned to die
        A servile death in servile company:
              Was ever grief like mine?

4   They part my garments, and by lot dispose
        My coat, the type of love, which once cured those
        Who sought for help, never malicious foes:
              Was ever grief like mine?

5   Nay, after death their spite shall further go;
        For they will pierce my side, I full well know;
        That as sin came, so Sacraments might flow:
              Was ever grief like mine?

6   But now I die; now all is finished.
        My woe, man's weal: and now I bow my head.
        Only let others say, when I am dead,
              Never was grief like mine.

Longing
OVERGANG

Barry Ferguson

Copyright © 2006 Barry Ferguson

1.   With sick and famished eyes,
      With doubling knees and weary bones,
            To thee my cries,
            To thee my groans,
      To thee my sighs, my tears ascend:
                No end?

2.   My throat, my soul is hoarse;
      My heart is withered like a ground
                Which thou dost curse.
                My thoughts turn round,
      And make me giddy; Lord, I fall,
                  Yet call.

3.   Look on my sorrows round!
      Mark well my furnace! O what flames,
              What heats abound!
              What griefs, what shames!
      Consider, Lord; Lord, bow thine ear,
                And hear!

4.   Behold, thy dust doth stir,
      It moves, it creeps, it aims at thee:
            Wilt thou defer
            To succour me,
      Thy pile of dust, wherein each crumb
                Says, Come?

5.   To thee help appertains.
      Hast thou left all things to their course,
            And laid the reins
            Upon the horse?
      Is all locked? hath a sinner's plea
                No key?

6.   My love, my sweetness, hear!
      By these thy feet, at which my heart
            Lies all the year,
            Pluck out thy dart,
      And heal my troubled breast which cries,
                Which dies.

Easter
RISE HEART

for Judy Rees

Barry Ferguson

Copyright © 2006 Barry Ferguson

The Dawning

Richard Shephard

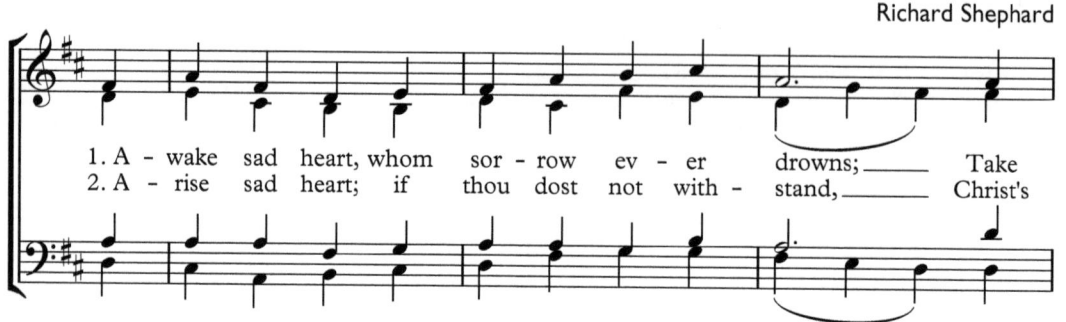

Copyright © 2007 The Royal School of Church Music

Whitsunday

Music: Grayston Ives (b 1948)

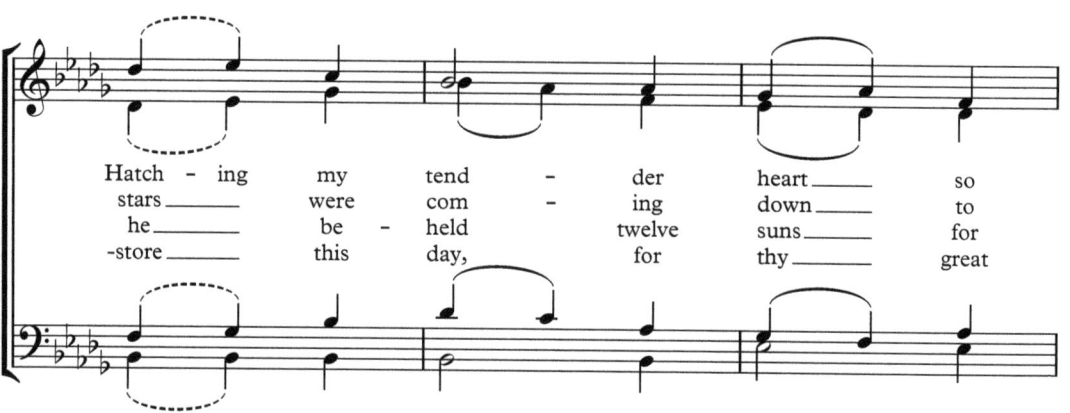

© 2007 The Royal School of Church Music. All Rights Reserved.

Trinity Sunday

LOWER BEMERTON

Barry Ferguson

Copyright © 2005 Barry Ferguson

1   Lord, who hast formed me out of mud,
      And hast redeemed me through thy blood,
      And sanctified me to do good;

2   Purge all my sins done heretofore:
      For I confess my heavy score,
      And I will strive to sin no more.

3   Enrich my heart, mouth, hands in me,
      With faith, with hope, with charity;
      That I may run, rise, rest with thee.

Sunday

Howard Moody

© 2007 Howard Moody

Originally composed in D flat

1
      O day most calm, most bright,
The fruit of this, the next world's bud,
Th' endorsement of supreme delight,
Writ by a friend, and with his blood;
The couch of time; care's balm and bay:
The week were dark, but for thy light:
      Thy torch doth show the way.

2
      The Sundays of man's life,
Threaded together on time's string,
Make bracelets to adorn the wife
Of the eternal glorious King.
On Sunday heaven's gate stands ope;
Blessings are plentiful and rife,
      More plentiful than hope.

3
      This day my Saviour rose,
And did inclose this light for his:
That, as each beast his manger knows,
Man might not of his fodder miss.
Christ hath took in this piece of ground,
And made a garden there for those
      Who want herbs for their wound.

4
      Thou art a day of mirth:
And where the week-days trail on ground,
Thy flight is higher, as thy birth.
O let me take thee at the bound,
Leaping with thee from sev'n to sev'n,
Till that we both, being tossed from earth,
      Fly hand in hand to heav'n!

A True Hymn

Howard Moody

© 2007 Howard Moody

1   My joy, my life, my crown!
       My heart was meaning all the day,
         Somewhat it fain would say:
       And still it runneth mutt'ring up and down
       With only this, *My joy, my life, my crown!*

2   Yet slight not these few words:
       If truly said, they may take part
         Among the best in art.
       The fineness which a hymn or psalm affords,
       Is, when the soul unto the lines accords.

3   He who craves all the mind,
       And all the soul, and strength, and time,
         If the words only rhyme,
       Justly complains, that somewhat is behind
       To make his verse, or write a hymn in kind.

4   Whereas if th'heart be moved,
       Although the verse be somewhat scant,
         God doth supply the want.
       As when the heart says (sigh'ng to be approved)
       O, could I love! and stops: God writeth, *Loved.*

Matins
BISHOP'S WALK

David Halls

1. I cannot ope mine eyes,
   But thou art ready there to catch
   My morning-soul and sacrifice:
   Then we must needs for that day make a match.

2. My God, what is a heart?
   Silver, or gold, or precious stone,
   Or star, or rainbow, or a part
   Of all these things, or all of them in one?

3. My God, what is a heart,
   That thou shouldst it so eye, and woo,
   Pouring upon it all thy art,
   As if that thou hadst nothing else to do?

4. Indeed man's whole estate
   Amounts (and richly) to serve thee:
   He did not heav'n and earth create,
   Yet studies them, not him by whom they be.

5. Teach me thy love to know:
   That this new light, which now I see,
   May both the work and workman show:
   Then by a sunbeam I will climb to thee.

Evensong

Howard Moody

Slow, like a Plainsong chant

1. Blest be the God of love, Who gave me eyes, and light, and power this day. Both to be busy, and to play. But
2. What have I brought thee home For this thy love? have I discharged the debt, Which this day's favour did beget? I
3. Yet still thou goest on. And now with darkness closest weary eyes, Saying to man, It doth suffice: Hence-

© 2007 Howard Moody

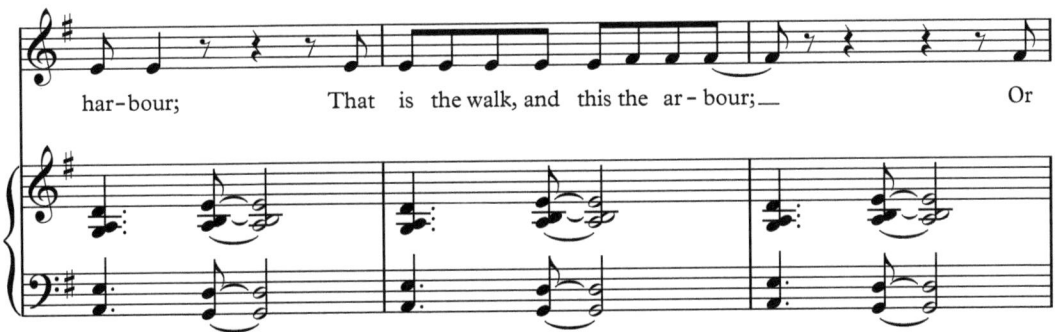

Perfection – The Elixir
SONG 20

Orlando Gibbons 1583-1625

1. Teach me, my God and King,
   In all things thee to see,
   And what I do in anything,
   To do it as for thee.

2. Not rudely, as a beast,
   To run into an action;
   But still to make thee prepossessed,
   And give it his perfection.

3. A man that looks on glass,
   On it may stay his eye,
   Or if he pleaseth, through it pass,
   And then the heav'n espy.

4. All may of thee partake;
   Nothing can be so mean
   Which with his tincture (for thy sake)
   Will not grow bright and clean.

5. A servant with this clause
   Makes drudgery divine:
   Who sweeps a room as for thy laws,
   Makes that and th' action fine.

6. This is the famous stone
   That turneth all to gold;
   For that which God doth touch and own
   Cannot for less be told.

The Pulley

Barry Ferguson

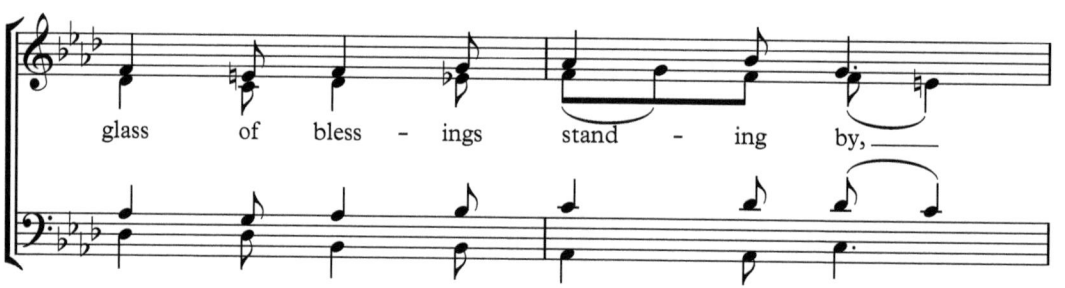

Copyright © 2007 Barry Ferguson

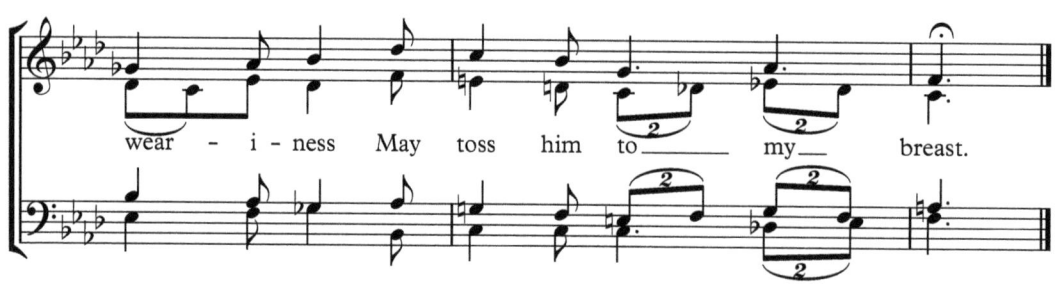

Gratefulness
PENRHYNDEUDRAETH

Edmund Hampton

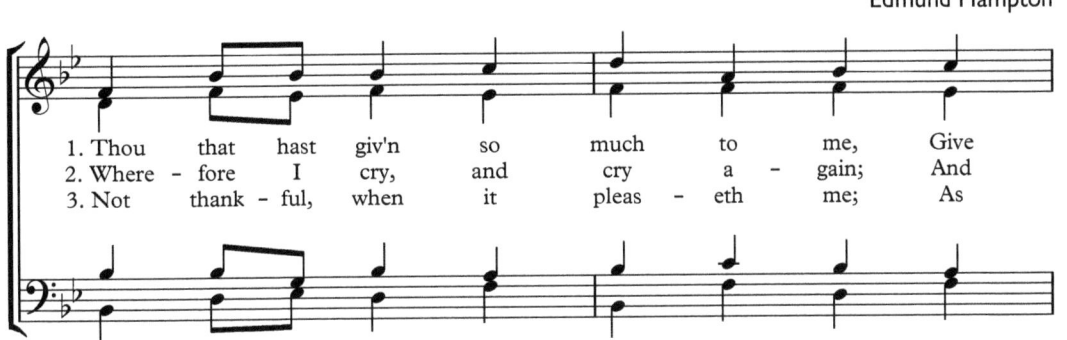

1. Thou that hast giv'n so much to me, Give
2. Where - fore I cry, and cry a - gain; And
3. Not thank - ful, when it pleas - eth me; As

one thing more, a grate - ful heart. See how thy beg - gar
in no qui - et canst thou be, Till I a thank - ful
if thy bless - ings had spare days: But such a heart, whose

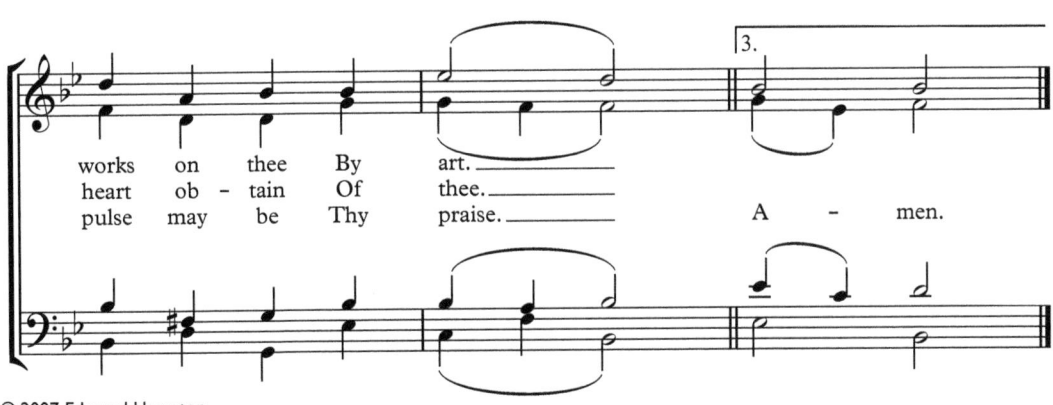

works on thee By art.
heart ob - tain Of thee.
pulse may be Thy praise. A - men.

© 2007 Edmund Hampton

The Flower

for Judy Rees

Alec Roth

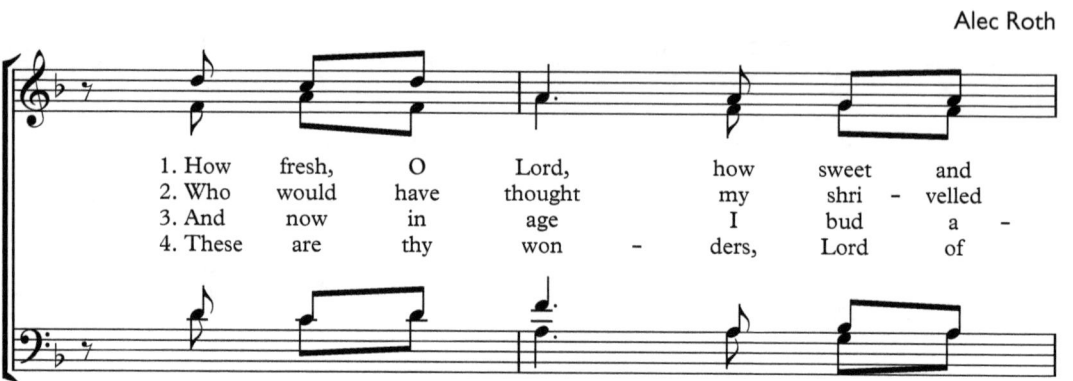

1. How fresh, O Lord, how sweet and
2. Who would have thought my shri - velled
3. And now in age I bud a -
4. These are thy won - ders, Lord of

clean Are thy re - turns! ev'n as the flowers in spring:
heart Could have re - cov - ered green - ness? It was gone
gain, Af - ter so ma - ny deaths I live and write;
love, To make us see we are but flowers that glide:

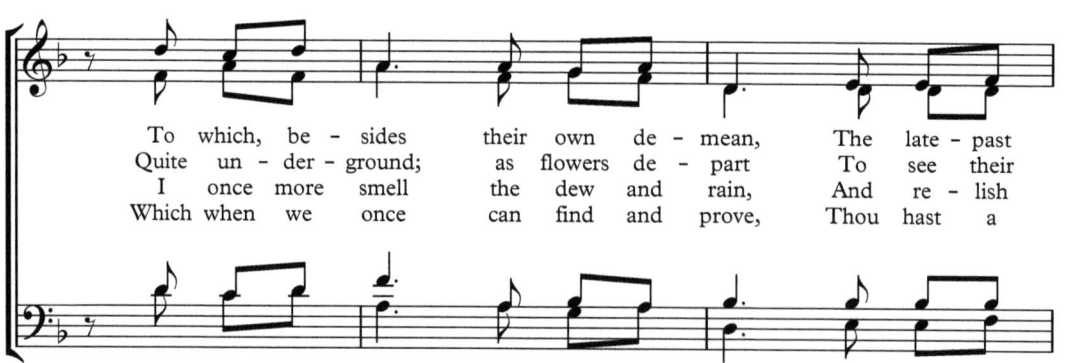

To which, be - sides their own de - mean, The late - past
Quite un - der - ground; as flowers de - part To see their
I once more smell the dew and rain, And re - lish
Which when we once can find and prove, Thou hast a

Copyright © 2007 Alec Roth

Advent

Discipline
Herbert appeals to God to take *the gentle path* in response to human frailty. It is the merciful love of God which will bring redemption, rather than *the man of war* picture of God. Herbert suffered from ill health, and there is a gentleness in his own understanding of human beings, expressed in verses 2 and 3, and in verse 4: *tho' I fail, I weep*.

Bitter-Sweet
A poem full of rueful humour about the paradoxical ways of God. It is the same God who casts down, yet sustains. With startling directness and intimacy, Herbert plays the same game: if that is how God does things, so can Herbert. Yet all is played out in the arena of the love of God and tremendous force falls on the last word *I will lament, and love*.

Christmas

Christmas*
Part of a longer poem where Herbert is the narrator, imagining himself as a traveller looking for lodging. So Christ is invited to find lodging in the human soul. *The rack* is both the manger holding provision for animals, and an instrument of torture with allusions to the cross of Christ. Herbert can't be silent when shepherds sing God's praise, and all his powers must *out-sing the daylight hours*.

Lent

Denial*
The soul is out of tune with God: God seems silent and far away. Words that do not rhyme at the end of each verse highlight the disharmony until the last verse, where *chime* and *rhyme* leave us upbeat.

Passiontide

The Sacrifice*
Christ is pictured as speaking to people from the cross. In a profoundly moving poem of 63 verses, the repeated question at the end of each verse *Was ever grief like mine?* is brought to a final conclusion *Never was grief like mine*. During Holy Week, groups of people have sat in George Herbert's little church of St Andrew's, Bemerton, reading this poem round verse by verse, and at the end, keeping silence.

Longing*
Herbert is earth bound and full of weariness and pain of body and spirit. Only God *my love, my sweetness* can bring healing and life. Fifty years after Herbert's death, Purcell set this text as a song, and chose the key of G minor. Barry Ferguson's tune *Overgang* is also in that key, in homage to Purcell.

Easter

*Rise Heart**
Bemerton's parson was an accomplished musician: heart and lute are called upon to praise the risen Lord in these verses, the first part of Herbert's beguiling poem *Easter*. But a further strand needs to be woven to *twist a song*: that of the Spirit who makes up *our defects with his sweet art*. The rich range of references in this tightly packed poem brings us to a contrapuntal climax of joy.
Calcined: reduce by burning
Vied: added to

The Dawning
With the dawning of Easter morning comes a clarion call to *awake* and *arise*. Sorrows can overwhelm us and earthly preoccupations drag us down, but Christ's resurrection can reverse the downward movement and lift us up with him. The unexpected image of the handkerchief is tenderly used, wiping tears and staunching wounds.

Pentecost

*Whitsunday**
A yearning for the *glorious gifts* and vibrant life of the Spirit which descended on the apostles at Pentecost. Even heavenly constellations were outshone by the light the apostles were bringing to the world. Old and New Testament allusions lie at the heart of this poem, as they do in much of Herbert's poetry. Bill Ives has adapted his anthem *Whitsunday* to form this hymn tune.

Trinity Sunday
Herbert must have relished finding words and form to write a poem on the Trinity. Three verses, each with three lines provide the basic form. In the first verse, he addresses God as creator-then as saviour and sanctifier. In the second, a plea to the second person of the Trinity. The third verse (with word triplets in each line) is a prayer for the sanctifying work of the Spirit. And is it fanciful to see in *run, rise, rest* another Trinitarian allusion?

Sunday

*Sunday**
Earth and heaven, Christ's death and resurrection, are brought together as Sunday is celebrated, a high spot in the week. It is a day of rest and joy, when the church, the bride of Christ, offers praise and receives nurture and blessing. Isaak Walton in his *Life of Mr. George Herbert*, wrote that on the Sunday before he died, Herbert rose from his bed, tuned his instruments, and sang and played the verse *The Sundays of man's life....*

A True Hymn
Words to sing praise to God may seem inadequate, yet God sees the loving intention of the heart of the worshipper and supplies what is lacking: he himself writes the word *loved*.

Morning

Matins
A sense of wonder lies at the heart of this poem. Every day the morning light brings a fresh chance to meet with God. This meeting brings us into a deeper relationship with a God who loves us *as if he has nothing else to do.*

Evening

Evensong
Looking back over the day, Herbert has experienced the love of God in active and passive times, however inadequate he feels his own response has been. This deepened sense of God's presence takes him to bed in peace.
Ebony box: night

General

Perfection – The Elixir
"Herbert rewrote this poem in a form that could be sung to Song 20. It is most likely intended to be sung to a solo voice accompanied by a lute or viol". Ben de la Mare.

The Pulley
Two things about this very original poem are startling. One is the image of the pulley as a means of connecting us with God. The other is the conceit that by withholding rest from his creation (for *our hearts are restless till they find their rest in thee* as Augustine understood) our loving Creator will draw us to himself.

*Gratefulness**
Edmund Hampton, a 16 year old pupil of Bishop Wordsworth's School, Salisbury has written this tune. The first two and last four lines of the poem make a delightful spoken prayer.

*The Flower**
Herbert gives a joyful response to the constant round of renewal and refreshment in the created world about him, seeing in it the impetus for a rediscovery of his own artistic creativity and spiritual health. The tune was composed by Alec Roth whilst he was staying at the Old Rectory, Bemerton in the Spring of 2007. In turn, it went on to form the core melodic inspiration of his choral work *Shared Ground*, a setting of texts by Vikram Seth which were themselves inspired by Herbert poems.
Demean: demeanour, bearing

* Extract from a longer poem

www.ingramcontent.com/pod-product-compliance
Ingram Content Group UK Ltd.
Pitfield, Milton Keynes, MK11 3LW, UK
UKHW051259180426
11947UKWH00020B/1804